I0109201

This Is How I Quit Smoking

By Mark Bonati

TMB Media, Copyright © 2016 by Mark Bonati
ISBN: 978-0-9958332-0-3 (paperback)

Thank you for purchasing this book. All rights are reserved under International Copyright Law. No part of this book may be reproduced or retransmitted in any form or by any means without permission in writing from the copyright owner.

Medical Disclaimer.
This book does *not* contain medical advice.

The content contained within this book is not to be considered professional, legal or medical advice and is to be used for personal entertainment purposes only. There is no guarantee, expressed or implied, that the information in this book will assist in the cessation of smoking. The author is not responsible or liable for any advice, treatment, or information that you obtain from this book.

The reader agrees that the information in this book is provided with the understanding that it is not designed to take the place of a physician. Diagnosis of any medical condition can only be carried out by a licensed physician. It is strongly recommended that the reader seeks out professional medical resources and advice from a licensed medical physician in regards to, but not limited to; stop smoking programs, exercise, diet, and the health complications associated with smoking.

All accounts, anecdotes and narratives contained within this book are true and chronicle real events. All names have been changed within the book in order to protect the identity and privacy of the people mentioned within the book.

I have written this book for you.

Because now it's your turn.

It's time.

Table of contents

Introduction

This is the story of how I quit smoking. A journal of sorts; how I went from being a heavy smoker, to freedom and life without cigarettes.

The first part of this book briefly describes my life as someone enslaved by cigarettes and the smoker's lifestyle. How addictive behavior had crept into every facet of my life, leaving me incapable of functioning without smoking.

The second part of the book chronicles the futility of my many failed attempts to quit smoking. Failures that left me overwhelmed and with a sense of hopelessness and remorse.

I think the picture I paint will be readily recognizable to anyone who's been there before. I move on to describe a period of self-examination that became the impetus for my steps toward freedom.

The people I met along the way had a profound effect on my ability to finally stop smoking. Some of their stories are tragic, some are triumphant. For me, all of them were influential.

Reading books about how to quit smoking, and I include this one, are an important and positive step towards breaking the habit.

But if it only took reading a book, I would've quit many years before I finally did.

I believe we tend to learn best when we're an active participant in the learning process. Especially if we can interact with people who've successfully walked the path we intend on taking.

I've always found it easier and more natural to grasp a concept when the teacher is right there with me. I liken it to the difference between sitting alone with a textbook, or sitting with a teacher.

A textbook may have all the answers. But it's the teacher who breathes life into those answers, bringing forth wisdom and understanding. Learning is an active process, and for me, talking to those who'd done it, who'd actually quit smoking and moved on with their life was central to my own success.

It's one thing to read about quitting cold turkey, the effective use of the patch, or following the steps in a stop smoking program.

It's something else to be able to sit down face to face and have a former smoker tell you, in specific detail, how they made it through the first 24 hours.

To be able to laugh with them at the sometimes comical antics we go through when in the midst of withdrawals. To hear a former smoker warn you about things like the 3 week itch, and more importantly the specific methods they used to overcome obstacles and move toward a smoke-free life.

All of those conversations and observations were the real catalyst that launched me in the direction of freedom.

Even all the past interactions I'd had with people who were not so positive, or whose words were unintentionally detrimental, became invaluable when I finally took the first steps to a life without cigarettes.

In the final part of this book, I put into steps the very things that helped me succeed. I write down, in point form, what I feel are the most important behaviors and actions I took on my journey out of the abyss of addiction.

I believe that those who've gone before have much to offer. And that's why I've written this book, to pass on what's been given to me.

How I took what I'd been given from others, and tailored it to my own circumstances. To offer up my own experiences as an inspiration and catalyst for change in other's lives.

It's my hope that you'll not only take on the challenge of quitting smoking because you want to move away from a negative and unhealthy way of life. But that you would aspire to a better and healthier life.

A life without cigarettes.

Chapter 1

I can resist anything except temptation.

Oscar Wilde

I was one of those guys.

No denial here, I was a full blown smoking addict. Every single aspect of my life and daily schedule revolved around smoking.

I left 10 minutes early for work every morning to make sure I could get in an extra smoke before I had to start. I sat near the exit when I went to a movie so I could have my cig lit that one minute earlier when the movie was over. In fact, I was lighting it as I walked through the exit door.

Life happened in between cigarettes.

I hated being an addict. I despised it, that I was a slave. But I won't lie. I enjoyed every single cigarette I ever smoked.

And there was a smoke for every occasion.

The first one in the morning: my *morning glory*. Nothing went better with a cup of coffee.

Coffee and cigarettes. Together they seemed to give me unmatched powers of mental focus. I could plan my day, untangle problems at work, discuss world issues, or repair a leaky faucet with complete and utter clarity.

There were the *social smokes*.

You have these on work breaks, in alleys outside wedding reception halls, 5 mandatory meters from entrances to places like hospitals and malls, in designated smoking areas, and in the few bars and coffee shops that still allow smoking.

The only prerequisite for a social smoke is to be in the vicinity of another smoker.

Two complete strangers could be standing at a bus stop. If one sparks up a cig and the other follows suit, there is an automatic bond between the two.

Conversation becomes easier with a stranger when cigarette smoke is in the air. Between friends, smoking is even better.

Then there was my *after dinner mint*. What better way to finish a meal off than with a cigarette.

Yes, a cigarette for every occasion. When I was stressed, they evened me out. When I was feeling a bit sluggish in the early afternoon, they gave me a shot of energy.

And driving, especially on long trips. There is no better way to stay awake when you're driving at night than to light one up.

Driving is when I smoked the most. I would fire one after the other down the hole until my lungs ached. Then I would light up another.

There are smokes. And then there are *really good* smokes. Like when you haven't had one for an hour or so. Nothing like quenching a raging nicotine fit.

And how about the; I just did something unusually stressful smoke? You know the one.

You just gave a speech at your best friend's wedding in front of 250 guests and all your jokes bombed.

Inhale all the way down to the furthest reaches of the bottom of your lungs and everything's back to A-OK.

There was something about cigarettes.

The way the tip would sort of back-flash when I lit it. The way I tap-butted the ash off the head in an ashtray, or rolled a cig in my fingertips.

Or the way I let it hang from my lips while I talked, letting the smoke drift up from my mouth as I spoke, stinging my eyes.

Yes, smoking. I hated being an addict. A slave.

But I loved all the rituals and all the comfort smoking was capable of providing.

The deadly pacifier.
I needed to quit.

Chapter 2

Happy New Year

Smokers are a sickly bunch.

Hacking and coughing, wheezing after a flight of stairs. The sound of gargling gravel when they laugh, spitting up nasty stuff every morning. The yellow fingers, receding gum lines and stained teeth. The smelly clothes. Even their cars stink inside.

All just a part of a long laundry list of necessary casualties required to feed the addiction. As long as it doesn't get too bad, all these things can be rationalized or ignored.

But what if you start getting sick? Suddenly it's harder to rationalize. I won't go into the details, but that's what started happening to me.

My Doctor had this look on his face when he told me to quit. And he wasn't asking, he was telling me to.

But how does one do this? I'd quit dozens of times before. The longest lasted about two months, but most attempts only lasted for a few days, maybe a week or two.

And I'd cheated every single time I quit, usually with cigars. I somehow rationalized that because they weren't cigarettes it was okay to smoke the occasional cigar, just to get me over the hump.

I tried everything over the years; nicotine gum, patches, smoking cessation medication, hypnosis, motivational tapes, cold turkey, and eating bags of sunflower seeds or countless lollipops to keep my fingers busy.

I read all sorts of 'quit smoking' material that discussed everything from self-motivation and the length of the average craving, to the psychology behind why I smoked in the first place. Yet a smoker I remained.

I needed to find a way.

It was the holiday season, so like many times before, I made quitting my New Year's resolution.

I believed that with these new health problems, I would finally have the motivation I needed to quit for good.

I also knew that I might as well keep smoking until New Year's Day because quitting before that would mean I would spend the holiday season going through withdrawals. Who wanted that? Not me. Certainly not those around me.

Without cigarettes, I became Mr. Evil. Short fuse? Nope. No fuse at all.

Without cigarettes time slowed to a crawl. A million nails dragged across a chalk board in my head, clouding my thoughts so much so that I became almost stupid. I would vacillate between uncontrollable rage and a tired, slow witted and clumsy lump.

No, there was no sense in going through that until after the holiday season was over.

And who's kidding who? I knew I wouldn't make it through all the upcoming social events with old friends without smoking.

So that was it. I had no real plan. I needed to quit and New Year's Day was to be quit day.

Although no one knew the extent of my health problems, I told all my friends that I was going to quit smoking. That's what you are supposed to do right? If you tell everybody, you're supposed to get motivation, affirmations, and a source of accountability.

I got the expected responses.

The non-smokers got all wide eyed and bubbly. They lectured me like some overly enthusiastic life coach;

"Oh, you'll never be so happy."

"You just need to keep up your determination and dedication. You can do it if you put your mind to it."

"Think of all the money you'll save, do you know that with the amount you spend on smoking you could take a really nice vacation every year, or make payments on a new car?"

No, really? Gee, that thought had never crossed my mind.

Or how about;
"Smoking is soooo stupid. I can't believe anyone still smokes with all we know about what it does to you, blah, blah, blah."

"Not to mention your clothes smell like smoke and it makes your teeth yellow. Yes, good for you! You can do it! And then you won't be guilty of spreading *all* that second hand smoke around either."

Many of these non-smokers will keep close tabs on you and your progress once you do quit.

Expect another wide-eyed big bubbly fan-fare if you've towed the line and remained smoke free.

But God forbid you tell them that you relapsed and had a few smokes during your first week or two. Complete disappointment. You might as well have just shot a puppy.

"Well…now you'll have to start all over. Doesn't it suck to go all those days smoke free, and then ruin your record? Now you know you can't count New Year's as your quit day, you'll have to start over. You are going to start over…. aren't you?"

The fact is, I think almost everyone relapses. It's part of the process of quitting. It's when relapses are not checked that… well, I'll get into that later.

It's not that the smokers are any better though.

While non-smokers may come across as annoying motivational speakers, smokers are the bitter cynics.

You see, a smoker does not celebrate the loss of a fellow smoking buddy.

Oh, they may give you some half-hearted encouragement, but underneath, I've found that many hope you fail.

"So how long do you think you'll make it this time?"
Or,
"What are you using, the patch or prescription drugs?"
That's actually pretty good encouragement coming from a smoker.

It's likely you'll get a negative reaction from some smokers when you tell them you're quitting.

I actually had one work associate get mad at me when I told him I was quitting because of health reasons.

"Everybody has to die from something" he snorted as he puffed on his cigarette.

How do you respond to something like that?

There's a brotherhood and sisterhood in knowing that you're doing something that's killing you, yet doing it anyway.

By quitting, you're admitting that the jig is up, that the smoking brotherhood is a farce, that the consequences can no longer be ignored or rationalized.

Many smokers will try to sabotage your efforts to quit. And more than likely these saboteurs will be your friends. Your *smoking* friends. They'll tease you. Sometimes bluntly, sometimes subtly.

They'll light up in front of you, inhale deeply, close their eyes and let out an;

"Aaahhhhhh, that's sooo good! Oh... but good thing you quit though, right?"

And if you're having a really bad nicotine craving, they won't mind letting you cheat by giving you 'Just one, to take the edge off'

Or sometimes they don't. Instead they try to punish you by lighting up in front of you, then saying dryly;

"Hey, I can't be the one that gets you off the wagon."

Okay, so maybe it's me that's being cynical here.

There are likely many people you know that will truly support your efforts to quit, smokers and non-smokers alike.

Many, many smokers have told me they wish they had the courage to try to quit and wished me well. And many, many non-smokers have been very supportive in my attempts to quit too.

But those negative reactions I mentioned do exist.

And it's those negative reactions that stand out when you're in the throes of nicotine detox. Those kinds of reactions do little to help you on your way.

I'm not going to get into a bunch of stuff in this book on how to deal with those reactions. Simpler and more effective is to remain aware that those types of negative reactions exist, and decide beforehand to not let them get to you.

You can make use of the non-smokers enthusiasm. And even later on, once you've proven yourself to the smokers, receive a grudging admiration for your ability to actually stop smoking. But that comes later. Long after bets with their friends on how long you'll last until you fall off the wagon have passed.

But I'm getting way ahead of myself.

I had eleven days before the big day. Eleven more days to smoke. I was going to make the most of those eleven days. As each day went by, I smoked a little more than usual because I knew quit day was coming.

That's how I always approached quitting. Doomsday was right around the corner. The closer to doomsday, the more I smoked.

I had two cigarettes before bed instead of one. I smoked like a steam engine when I was out with friends.

I was probably smoking 9 or 10 more cigarettes per day than usual. And New Year's Eve? That day and evening I smoked twice as many cigarettes as I normally would in a day.

At 2 a.m. I smoked the last cigarette from my pack right down to the nub. I inhaled as deeply as possible and butted it out.

"I quit, happy New Year"

New Year's Day. I woke up at about 9 am, feeling absolutely terrible. I'd smoked more the previous night than I normally would in two days. The first thing I thought about when I woke up was coffee and a smoke.

Oh yeah. Dammit! Today is quit day. I went and put on the coffee, took some painkillers, and stuck a nicotine patch on my arm.

By 1pm, I was grinding my teeth and flicking an imaginary cigarette in my fingers. Some nicotine gum temporarily eased the craving. I rubbed the nicotine patch on my arm, trying to get it to release its nectar. It just got itchy.

That evening, I went and played some billiards with friends. Questions abounded, "How are you doing? Are you going crazy yet?" The smokers lit up and smiled. I had a massive headache. But still, I'd made it through the first day.

Day 2. Hardly any sleep the night before. I put on a nicotine patch as soon as I got up, then I made coffee.

Back to work today. I still followed the routine of going with my work mates to their smoke break. Instead of a cigarette, I had yet another coffee and a piece of nicotine gum, all the while rubbing the hell out that seemingly useless patch and watching everybody else smoke. Again, listening to all the comments, watching them smoke, smelling the smoke.

I watched them inhale, gazed at the red hot cherry glowing at the end of their cigarettes. I could just claw the walls.

An endless supply of toothpicks gave my restless fingers something to do. My headache had not gone away despite several painkillers. My skin seemed to crawl.

As the nicotine from the gum and patch began to find its way into my system, the anger and frustration welling inside me eased. I drank cup after cup of coffee. I could hardly concentrate on anything. Smoking, or the lack thereof, was the only thing on my mind.

By afternoon, I could take it no more.

I asked a smoker for a drag of his cigarette. Then I decided to have just one and damn the expected comments. I bummed a cig and smoked it right down to the filter.

It was soooo good. It felt like the vice grip on my head had loosened a bit. I immediately wanted another but was too embarrassed to ask.

The following days were not much better. My temper worsened and I would rage and curse at cars that didn't signal before changing lanes. Even television commercials would set me off. They were either too long, or just plain annoying. And watching anyone on television that smoked brought instant cravings.

I couldn't sleep at night, and despite drinking 2 or 3 pots of coffee per day, I was exhausted all the time.

I found myself hanging out with my smoking friends more than usual, just so I could bum a cigarette or two.

"It won't be long now." they would chuckle.

I searched through jacket pockets to find old cigarette packs that might contain a cig or two.

After 5 days, my cheating was getting out of hand. I decided something had to be done. I decided to smoke one cigar per day. Not the fat ones, just those skinny cigarillos.

I bought a pack and would smoke them in private. That way I could avoid all the comments from friends and co-workers.

I'd smoke part of a cigarillo in the morning, put it out, smoke a bit more at noon, and the rest on the way home from work. They didn't really relieve the cravings, but at least I was going through the motions of smoking.

By the end of the first week, I felt like I was living in a nightmare. I could take it no more.

I was driving down the street and the next thing I knew, I was at a gas station buying cigarettes. Like a giddy child at Christmas, I could hardly wait to open the pack.

Three consecutive cigarettes later, reality set in. It was over. I'd lost.

I felt like I had this curse that I couldn't get rid of. And every failed attempt to quit compounded that curse with a feeling of failure, remorse and hopelessness.

I promised myself I would wean myself off them slowly, using the patch and gum to help me at least lower the number of cigs I smoked every day.

Yeah right.

The only thing left to face was the embarrassment of lighting up in front of friends and co-workers.

Chapter 3

Normal

I'm in the emergency ward of the hospital with wires and tubes hooked up all over me. After several hours, the doctor tells me he's admitting me so they can run further tests.

It's about 3 am and I'm moved from the emergency ward and placed in a bed in a large room. There are three other beds in the room, all of them occupied with sleeping patients.

After the nurse reattaches all the hoses and wires and checks my blood pressure, she leaves the room.

It's almost dark except for a dim light in the hallway. Hospital sounds emanate from down that hallway. I'm feeling very, very vulnerable.

Normal is just down that hall. It's just down the hall, two levels down the elevator, through the sliding glass security doors and past the friendly nurse in admitting.

Normal is just outside those hospital doors that lead to the outside world where everybody in Normal is taking their life for granted. I very much want to return to my Normal life.

One of my new room-mates is not asleep.

He's muttering something about needing to get horses back in a barn as he crawls out of bed and attempts to change into his street clothes and stumbles around the room in the dark.

Nurses arrive to investigate the commotion and put the elderly gentleman back to bed, returning the oxygen tubes back on his nose.

Sleep doesn't come for me at all that night.

 I spend the next three days getting to know my roommates, and of course, undergo several tests.

Joe is in the bed next to mine. I'd guess that Joe is in his mid-fifties. His sister tells me he used to be a construction worker. She visits Joe every day.

Joe had a massive stroke a while back.

Every morning, hospital aids come in and get Joe out of bed, change his diaper, and give him a bath. Then they strap him upright in a secure chair where he waits for nurses to come and feed him.

Joe tries his best to reach for the water cup with the straw because he's very thirsty. Unfortunately the once skilled hands of a tradesman cannot even grasp a plastic cup, and all he can do is grunt until someone holds the straw up to his dry diabetic mouth. I still pray for Joe.

The bed across from me contains Frank. I never do find out exactly what's wrong with Frank. He's a retired farmer and well into his seventies. He's also very kind and polite, although he sometimes forgets where he is, and often wanders around the room at night, muttering about lost horses.

John is in the bed next to Frank. He's also in his seventies. I find out he's a retired ranch hand, and when he laughs, which is often, it sounds like a combination of a milkshake being slurped up a straw, and a dragon gargling cannon balls.

There's only so much you can talk about under these circumstances, each of us confined to our beds by wires and air tubes. John, Frank and I compare the settings to our oxygen supply valves. John's is highest, "at seven" he says, morbidly triumphant.

Frank can leave the room for short walks down the hall without his oxygen. John can't and complains to the nurse; he wants a portable bottle.

John asks me if I smoke. Then he tells me that smoking cigars and the straw-dust from working in grain elevators and on ranches have ruined his lungs. He doesn't admonish me for smoking though. I think he just came from a different generation. Some things just are the way they are.

Joe's sister visits. My friends and family visit. Frank and John's wives and grandchildren visit. I am wheeled around the hospital for various tests.

When the wives of Frank and John visit, there's an uncomfortable tension in the room. I see a nervousness in those women's eyes. They stand beside the bed of their loved one, holding their hand and forcing a smile that betrays their attempts to hide their fear.

I understand what those women are worried about. Their Normal is threatened. Sad changes are inevitable.

Just when I begin to think the doctors have ignored all my pleas to be released, one walks in and tells me I can go home.

Oh, I'm not done yet. There are plenty more tests to come, more visits to the emergency ward. But for now, I can go home.

I walk out those glorious doors to Normal. I'm feeling very happy, like I've been given a pardon, a second chance. I walk outside smiling.

Then it hits me. I smell it.

A girl in her early twenties, dressed in her hospital gown, slippers and winter jacket is outside smoking a cigarette, 5 mandatory meters from the hospital door.

I hadn't had bad nicotine cravings while I was in there, even when John and I talked about smoking.

Maybe it'd been all that oxygen. Maybe because I'd been too nervous and scared about what those tests were going to show and how I'd vowed to myself a 1000 times that now I would quit.

But there it was; the smell of cigarette smoke.

I hated myself.
I wanted one.

Chapter 4

Everybody quits

Get rid of all your vices by the time you're thirty.

Wise words I'd heard while I was still in my twenties.
And I did, for the most part. The only vice still
hanging around was the smoking.

But now I'm 40.

I decided to call an old friend. We'd done some
rebel rousing together when we were young. Him
more so than me.

When we were teenagers, he used to wear this
t-shirt with the words;
I'll try anything once....maybe twice!

He lived by that motto, and by his own admission,
was an addiction magnet. He had a type-A
personality and did everything on maximum
overdrive; work, women, fighting, and hard partying.

Most of his twenties were spent on full tilt. Most
people that live like he did are dead or in jail. A few
of the people he hung around with back then are
dead.

By the grace of God, he got help in his early thirties, and he quit everything. He quit the drugs, the alcohol, the smoking, and a self-destructive lifestyle that very few could ever match.

So I asked him how he did it. How he beat all those monsters that had their hooks in so deep.

"Everybody quits," he told me "It's just a matter of how much you want to have left when you finally do."

I've never been to an AA or drug counselling meeting, so I don't know if that's where he got that line from, but it struck home.

"Bottom is different for everybody," he began.

"You can hit bottom early, if you're lucky. You know how far down the hole I was before I said *enough*. It doesn't get much lower than that."

"I'm very fortunate to even be here. In fact, for years I just assumed I'd be dead before my thirtieth birthday."

"As far as smoking, well for some people maybe their vanity kicks in. They see some wrinkles and premature aging, and boom. That's it, that's their bottom. They find a way to quit."

"You can quit smoking now, and try to salvage your health, maybe even regain your health."

"Maybe you'll wait till it costs you a lung, or until any number of diseases shows up, and you have to go through some god awful suffering and pain before you say enough.

Or….or maybe you'll keep making excuses and wait until it's too late and it takes everything from you."

"And they'll put you in a box in the ground and those cigarettes will have robbed you of all the good times you could've had, all the things you could have accomplished and experienced.

But in a sense, you will have finally quit. Only there'll be nothing left to lose at that point."

He continued;

"Like I said, everybody quits. It really is a matter of how much you want to have left when you do"

"So bottom is up to you. You decide."

His words stayed in my head. Eventually smoking would likely kill me. I held the power to end the addiction. I just needed to decide that I had a life worth living without cigarettes, and that it'd be worth going through the pain of quitting to get to that life.

How many smokers do you know that say they're going to quit…someday? Probably most. You've probably said that yourself many times. I think we all have.

I know this carpenter, a heavy smoker. He used to say to me;

"I wish my doctor would tell me that I need to quit, that my life depends on it. Then I'd finally have the motivation to quit."

Hmmmm. So far my doctor hasn't told me my life depends on quitting. But he's been testing me for all sorts of things, trying to get to the bottom of my illness.

When your doctor starts talking about testing your white blood cell count, you sit up and take notice.

My parents had been friends with this married couple, Sue and George, for many decades.

They'd planned on spending their retirement years travelling the world. When they turned 65, they finally retired and looked forward to putting their travel plans into action. But a few months after retirement, Sue got sick.

She was a lifelong smoker, and the prognosis was not good. Sue had lung cancer and immediately went into cancer treatment.

But even facing death, she just couldn't quit smoking.

Tragically, Sue is gone now. She's finally stopped smoking though. But she lost everything.

Of course you've probably heard many sad stories like this before. I know just as well as anyone that hearing these stories is not necessarily enough to motivate a smoker to quit. The addiction is just that powerful.

But the words of my childhood friend echoed in the back of my head;

What do you want to have left when you quit?

Because you will quit. Everybody quits.

You will decide where bottom is and how much you are going to allow the addiction to take from you.

Chapter 5

Man with a plan

The lying was over. There were no more excuses. I had to quit, it was just that simple.

At first this was extremely depressing because I'd failed so many times before that I really didn't know how I was going to do it.

It seemed senseless to make yet another attempt to quit if I was just going to do the same thing as all the other times. That always led to failure.

So I took a step back. I looked at myself from the outside in. I took out a notebook and started writing things down. These are some of the many questions I asked myself;

What were the things that made me want to smoke?

What times and places did I have daily ritual or habit smokes?

What parts of my life were closely associated with smoking?

Which people did I mainly associate with because of smoking? Where did I interact with these people?

What places did I go to where I would be likely to smoke?

Then I took a look at my previous attempts to quit. These are some of the questions I asked myself about that:

In my past attempts to quit, how had I prepared for quitting in the weeks prior to 'quit day'?

After I quit, which days were the worst for withdrawal symptoms? What time of day seemed to be worst?

What did I feel like when I went through withdrawals? Were these feelings at least partially controllable?

What stop-smoking aids had I used? Which ones had offered me real relief? Why did I think they offered me that relief? Was the way I was using them helping me break my nicotine addiction, or just the daily habits and rituals of smoking? Was I only using them to ease withdrawal symptoms?

What reaction did people have when I tried to quit? Did their reactions affect my attempts to quit?

What caused me to fail in the past? Other smokers? Cheating? Weak willpower?

I filled several pages with notes. It was strange, but as I wrote things down, I began to feel empowered.

By seeing my addictive behavior on paper, it was easier to see where I was making mistakes. Some of it seemed obvious. A few things jumped off the page.

For example, in all my previous attempts to quit, I had always looked at quit day as doomsday. Consequently, I smoked more and more the closer quit day came. By the time quit day arrived, my daily nicotine consumption was considerably higher than normal.

I looked at the list of people I smoked with. One of my friends in particular stood out on the list.

He used to quit smoking for 8 months at a time. But the whole time, he would be on the nicotine patch, afraid to wean himself off nicotine completely. Then, something would happen; a night out with the boys or some life emergency, and he'd be smoking again.

He lived like that for years; smoker, non-smoker, but never a non-addict.

It struck me. In all my previous attempts to quit, the focus had never been on breaking the actual addiction to nicotine. I'd always tried to break the habit of smoking, the mental addiction. I'd continued to use nicotine through patches and gum, while trying to replace the habit of smoking with things like toothpicks, sunflower seeds, candy and coffee.

What if I did it differently this time?

What if my initial focus was centered on breaking the nicotine addiction first, and then working on the addictive mental and behavioral patterns after?

What if I freed my body of nicotine? Make that the primary focus. Instead of focusing on my mental addiction and trying to find substitutes for the smoking rituals as I'd done in the past, what if I focused on breaking the physical addiction first?

What if I quit torturing myself with the nicotine patch and gum and cigars and cheat smokes? What if I just went through a self-inflicted detox to get it over with?

And what if I didn't try to find substitutes for the rituals of smoking? Just remove those habits and rituals altogether.

A complete clean break from anything related to smoking. No more toothpicks, sunflower seeds or candy to keep my fingers busy. No more hanging around other smokers or places where smoking is prevalent. A clean break from the smoker's lifestyle.

But isn't that just the same as quitting cold turkey? Maybe not.

I started formulating a plan. I looked at my notes and identified weaknesses. I came up with ideas on how I would overcome each of those weaknesses.

It started coming together. It seemed a little more possible, like I finally had a map.

I used to know this older gentleman, a life-long heavy smoker. For several decades, his daily routine included an early morning trip to the coffee shop for coffee and cigarettes with his close life-long friends before he went to work every day.

When smoking was banned in restaurants, he and his friends moved their early morning routine to a coffee shop with a picnic table out front. They'd get their coffee in go-cups and sit out front of the coffee shop and drink their coffee and smoke while sitting at the picnic table.

When the cold winter months came, they'd get their coffee, then they'd all get into one of their cars and sit there smoking, drinking coffee, and socializing.

When his health began to fail, his doctor told him that the cigarettes had to go.

"There is **no way** you're taking my cigarettes away from me! No. Way." He angrily snapped.

It wasn't just that he didn't want to give up cigarettes.

For him, very important life routines and social structures were attached to smoking. He knew his friends were never going to quit, and quitting would mean he'd either have to sit there and suffer while his friends smoked around him, or give up his deeply embedded social routines.

He was absolutely unwilling to make any changes to his life routine and he smoked until the end.

I realized that if I wanted to succeed, I would need to be **willing** to upset the apple cart and make some big changes to my routine.

In the past, I'd had a victim mentality every time I tried to quit smoking. I felt sorry for myself and spent a lot of time and energy focusing on how bad quitting was making me feel.

Because I spent most of my time focused on how lousy I felt, every other area of my life turned upside down. I was grumpy and on edge all the time, so I yelled at people in traffic and was edgy around friends and family.

Withdrawals made it hard to concentrate which made work seem harder. Instead of focusing my efforts toward quitting and finding solutions to these problems, I had only focused on how miserable I felt.

At times, I admit I was almost childlike in my attitudes and actions when I was quitting. Like a child having a tantrum because his mother won't allow him to have candy.

If I was ever going to quit smoking, I needed to stop feeling sorry for myself, lose the victim mentality and take control of my life.

I started talking to a lot of other people who'd successfully quit smoking. I asked them how they quit. I wouldn't let them get away with giving me a one or two line answer either.

I wanted specifics.

I wanted to know what they did the night before they quit, what they ate, which days were worst and how long before it started getting easier.

I asked them what it was that got them over the hump. I picked their brains and asked about the sticking points they encountered when they were going through the process of quitting, and how they overcame these obstacles to reach success.

Some of the advice they gave me was fantastic. They took these little tidbits of information for granted, yet I recognized them as a solution to my own fight for a smoke-free life.

It was inspiring. There is nothing quite as motivating as listening to someone who has successfully gone down the road before you.

I have to admit that I smoked many cigarettes while I worked out this plan.

"Hell," I thought "Cigarettes have the power to give me all this mental focus, I might as well smoke my way to a quit plan."

I'm not proud of that part, but it is what it is.

The good news was that I finally had a pretty good idea what I was going to do next.

Chapter 6

The weeks before

I had decided that the upcoming April Fool's Day would be a good day to quit. Almost poetic in fact, as I'd been such a fool to ever start.

That gave me several weeks to prepare. I nicknamed this stage the Weed-less Wednesdays and Wean down stage.

Since I'd identified that in past attempts to quit, I'd always smoked more the closer quit day came, I decided a change was in order. I would wean my daily cigarette count down so that when I quit, the withdrawals would hopefully be more manageable.

The first thing I did was lower my daily cigarette consumption down to 20 cigarettes per day. You can do this through sheer willpower for a day or two, but falling back into the old habit is all but inevitable without a structured routine.

Normally I'd buy cigarettes on impulse. I kept packs all over the place, just in case I did run out. And when I ran out, I bought more, simple as that. But that wouldn't work here because it's too easy to lose count of how many I'd had, and too easy to cheat. So I went out and bought a carton. Every morning, I would count out 20 cigarettes, put them in a pack, and take them with me.

Now every smoker gets really miserly with their smokes if they're running low. There's no handing out smokes to those that want to bum one if you've only got a few left in your pack.

And when you're running low, you only tend to smoke them when you absolutely need them, when the craving really hits.

That's how I looked at it. I only had so many cigs to make it through the day, so I rationed them. Instead of having two smokes on a smoke break, I'd only have one. Then I'd immediately go back to work so I wouldn't have to watch anyone else smoke.

I started rationing how much time I spent with my smoking friends too. If they asked about it, I was just 'a bit busy.'

I started avoiding things and places that I strongly associated with smoking, like the pool hall or the coffee shop with the picnic table set up outdoors especially for smokers.

Every week, I lowered the number of cigarettes I would take each morning by two. So the second week I took 18 cigs per day, and the third week it was 16 per day, etc.

I knew I could make it a few days without cigarettes without having a total meltdown. The trip to the hospital showed me that. So I wanted to try to reproduce that abstinence, one day per week. Not only to lower my dependence on cigarettes, but to get myself mentally toughened up, so that when quit day came, it wouldn't be such a shock.

There's a yearly event in Canada called National Non-Smoking Week and they call the Wednesday of that week Weed-less Wednesday. You try to make it through Wednesday without smoking. It wasn't National Non-Smoking Week, but I was going to try to implement Weed-less Wednesdays into my plan.

The biggest problem I had with this idea of Weed-less Wednesday was the mental thought of going a whole day without smoking. The thought of voluntarily going a full day without smoking just grated against my nerves.

I came up with an idea. 24 hours is technically the same as one day. If I stopped smoking at 12 noon on Wednesday and lit up at 12 noon on Thursday, I had technically gone one day without smoking.

Doing it this way meant I would only have to make it through half of Wednesday without smoking. Not too much problem there.

When I woke up Thursday morning, I was definitely in desperate need of a smoke. But waiting until noon Thursday was also manageable, although I admit most of the morning was spent looking at my watch, counting down the hours.

The first time I did this, I felt a real surge of success. My confidence was beginning to grow, and quitting seemed like quitting might actually be possible.

Momentum was building.

Chapter 7

Draining the swamp

Let me ask you a question.

In any of your past attempts to quit smoking, have you ever felt overwhelmed? Not just by the nicotine withdrawals, but by everything else in your life?

Like, you somehow picked the worst possible time to try to quit smoking because the day after you quit, some sort of life-crisis emerged.

Your boss moved the deadline of the big project up. The kitchen faucet started leaking all over the floor just as you were about to take the kids to school in the morning. The car breaks down, or some large unexpected bill arises. The list is endless.

It seems like fate is working against you and now is just not the right time to be trying to quit. There's just too much going on, and the stress of quitting and going through nicotine withdrawal will be too much to handle right now.

Not only that, but you start asking yourself the question;

Is my life really going to be all that much better without smokes?

I mean really, things aren't all that bad yet and I'm managing to get by. And if I try to quit, I'm eventually just going to relapse and start smoking again, so why put myself through all that misery. Especially now, with everything that's going on in my life.

If you're anything like me, then your answer to those questions will be yes. Quitting seems overwhelming and there's always some sort of life emergency that pops up just when you want to quit.

There's an old saying:

When you're up to your ass in alligators, the first thing you do is drain the swamp.

So how does that apply to quitting smoking? Well, first let's look at life's crises and how I handled them as a smoker in the past.

To put it bluntly, smoking was my crutch. I felt that with a cigarette in my mouth I could focus and solve any problem. If I just took the time for a smoke, I could come up with the correct solution to any of life's problems.

My whole life was structured, in one form or another, around smoking. My daily schedule. When I left for work in the morning. The friends I spent the most time with. The places where I spent my free time. Most of my life happened in between cigarettes.

So really, it's not much of a surprise that my life seemed to be going off the rails whenever I tried to quit in the past.

It was clear that if I was going to succeed, I'd not only have to stop smoking and break my physical and mental addiction to cigarettes. I would also have to make a break from my life routine.

I needed something definite; a clear interruption in my daily pattern of living.

It would mean a change in the places I hung out at. A change in the way I handled problems. A change in the amount of time and the places I would spend with smokers. A change in just about every sense of my daily routine.

No more cigarettes on the drive to work in the morning. No more smoke breaks at work. No more friendly smoking and coffee get-togethers with friends.

The idea of changing my whole lifestyle seemed daunting. But I needed to drain the swamp, so to speak, so I could focus on beating the alligator.

When I quit this time, I wanted to have a definite break in my daily pattern, my life routine. A disconnect from the way I lived as a smoker, and a new way of living as a non-smoker. Especially during those first few critical days and weeks after I quit smoking, when I would be up to my neck in nicotine withdrawals.

I needed to be away from anything and anyone that could cause problems or temptations.

The 3 days I spent in the hospital had got me thinking as I planned all this out. Why hadn't I gone through such bad withdrawals while I was in there?

Was it really all the oxygen? Was it just the circumstances? How could I reproduce that?

After all, the first 3 days were always the absolute worst days for withdrawals when I had tried to quit in the past. By day four I would usually be cheating, if not a full relapse.

Then I recognized something else about my previous attempts to quit. Aside from being extremely irritable, I was always very, very tired. Exhausted, lethargic and mentally slow.

I did spend a lot of my time sleeping while I was in the hospital. What could I do to get over those first lethargic, tiresome days after I quit?

I recalled a scene from a movie I'd watched years ago, where the main character, a drug addict, basically locks himself in his bedroom to detox himself from drugs.

Hmmmm. Not a bad concept.

Remove yourself from all the stresses of daily life and all sources of temptation until the worst of the cravings are over.

No, I didn't want to lock myself in my bedroom for a week, but I could do something else instead.

One of the guys I'd talked to who'd successfully quit smoking had done something similar. He had holed up in his house for a few days until the worst of the cravings were over.

He avoided all the temptations and stresses of the outside world until he got over the worst of the nicotine withdrawals.   I decided that I'd design my own version of detox.

I realized that there were many, many things in the way I lived with the potential to tempt me and act as stumbling blocks to my beating the addiction. My lifestyle was kind of like my own personal swamp. And my cigarette addiction was the biggest alligator in my swamp. I knew what I needed to do;

Drain the swamp and take the alligator head on.

I decided that once I quit smoking, I'd change every aspect of my life that I could control. I'd either remove things that caused temptation, remove myself from the temptation, or develop new ways to handle myself in the face of temptation.

My daily routine was going to change. The amount of time I hung around smokers was going to change. Drastically. The way I took care of myself was going to change.

Life was going to happen and it wasn't going to be between cigarettes anymore.

I wanted to drain the swamp, get rid of the alligators, and move on with life. Life without cigarettes.

I vowed to get myself healthy again. When I was young, I played every sport available. I'd been an athlete in high school and had remained an avid exercise enthusiast in my college years. I would recommit myself to exercise and to eat properly and beat whatever illness the doctors were testing me for.

I'd always been a worry wart; obsessing and stressing about everything all the time. So I decided it was time to put more happiness and laughter back into my life too.

Laughter is the best medicine they say. In the future I'd watch comedies and read joke books and not take everything so seriously. I'd look at the lighter side of life and find things that bring genuine happiness. That's something that'd been sorely missing in my life for a long, long time.

April 1st was only a few days away. Strange thing, I wasn't freaking out about it. I was almost looking forward to it. I wanted to see if what I had planned out next would work.

Several times I'd been able to wean myself down to 12 cigarettes per day. I couldn't do it every day, but even so, I was smoking way less than normal.

I found I couldn't make it on less than 12 without going squirrely, but 12 was still significantly lower than my normal daily habit.

I had several weed-less Wednesday/Thursdays (24 hr. periods) under my belt. In fact, the week before, I had made an actual whole Wednesday without smoking.

Friday arrived, my last day to smoke. I was nervous, but not in the usual panic. I hadn't told anyone of my plan to quit. In fact no one even really noticed that I was smoking way less than usual.

Aside from my doctor, I had no intention of telling anyone that I was quitting. At least not for now. I just didn't want that mental burden and all the comments and expectations.

Not yet. If I made it, great, I would tell people once I felt strong enough. But if I failed, I wouldn't have to explain myself to anyone either.

I'm definitely not saying that's the way anyone else should do it. Many people trying to quit smoking get a tremendous boost from the support and accountability of an outside support network. But that method had just not worked for me in the past.

The knowledge that I wouldn't have to face anyone's disappointment or expectations took a huge burden off my mind. I could focus my energy on the task at hand.

A few friends asked what I was doing over the next weekend. At this point, I considered these smoking buddies of mine to be alligators in my swamp.

So I told them I was going to be busy with some projects around the house, and I wouldn't be available this weekend. I quietly made sure that there'd be no interruptions this weekend unless it was an absolute emergency.

I wasn't leaving the house for the duration of the weekend. It was to be my own intervention. My own personal detox. I was focused on breaking my addiction to nicotine. Free my body and my mind will follow. That's what I was hoping anyway.

I planned on watching a bunch of movies over the weekend. On the way home from work, I stopped at the grocery store and bought several bags of chips, soda, pretzels, peanuts, etc. This weekend was going to be tough, so I wouldn't deny myself of anything that I wanted.

For this weekend and this weekend only, I would eat what I wanted, whenever I wanted to eat it. I knew that I'd be removing nicotine, so having a temporary form of indulgence in the form of junk food was mentally reassuring.

Normally if I was quitting, I'd wait until late at night to have my last cigarette. I'd smoke my farewell cigarette right before bed.

I used to treat it as if it were some sort of ceremony, like I was saying goodbye to a close friend.

This time I had my last smoke at 7 p.m. There were still two left in the pack when I threw them in the garbage, along with the remaining full packs from the carton. At the time, it seemed almost inconsequential.

I spent the next hour going through the house and my pickup truck. Anything smoking related, like lighters and ashtrays, went into the garbage. I didn't want to be stumbling across a half pack of cigarettes in some jacket pocket in the weeks to come when I'd surely be in a state of withdrawal and weakness.

I ordered some pizza for supper, lied down on the couch and watched a movie. I was asleep by midnight.

I slept in Saturday morning. After making breakfast and having a coffee, I returned to the couch and popped another movie in. By noon I was definitely craving a cigarette. But I was used to this feeling from all the previous weeks of weed-less Wednesdays, so the craving was manageable.

In past attempts to quit, I would've been drinking all kinds of coffee to keep me alert all day. All that caffeine would then compound the feelings of panic and aggravate the cravings even more.

Instead, I avoided any further coffee after breakfast. I just allowed the feeling of lethargy that accompanies withdrawal to run its course.

When I was tired I slept. I munched on junk food, watched movies, and slept some more. It didn't matter that I was mentally slowing down or getting edgy. The only thing on my agenda was watching movies, eating junk food, and sleeping.

No job stress, no outside temptations, no driving through traffic. No exposing myself to anything that might set me off. I had a supply of nicotine gum and patches waiting, just in case the cravings got out of control.

"I am not *trying* to quit, I *am* quitting. I am *going to* beat this."

I kept that thought running through my head.

"I am going to beat this!'

I spent the whole day watching TV and taking it easy.

Sunday morning was not so easy. I woke up with a massive headache, and that feeling of nails on a chalk board type of craving. I took some painkillers, ate a bowl of cereal, and lied down on the couch again. I was tired of watching movies though, and just stared at the ceiling.

"Here it comes." I thought, "Here comes the ugly part."

I considered putting a nicotine patch on. Too lazy to get up, I just laid there, arguing the pros and cons of putting on a nicotine patch.

I analyzed how I was feeling. Like, exactly how I was feeling, and where. From my toes to my nose, I did a complete inventory of just how my body was feeling. Normally those uncomfortable feelings of withdrawal would make me feel panicked.

With my eyes closed, I envisioned this giant ugly brown ball, full of thorns.

Is that what this addiction monster looks like? Instead of panicking, and instead of fighting the lousy feelings and all the cravings, I just laid there and let it happen.

I let the cravings wash all over me, while I analyzed exactly how they were making me feel, top to bottom, inside and out. Eventually I fell asleep.

When I woke up an hour later, my head was still pounding.

Completely sick of eating junk food, I decided to make a trip to the grocery store. I went to the produce section and filled my cart up with anything that looked colorful and healthy.

Returning home, I went to the kitchen and made a big vegetable salad and a fruit salad. It felt good to be eating healthy food, and seemed to fit into this mindset of becoming addiction free and living a healthier life.

But the cravings didn't abate and those feelings of frustration and anger returned. I decided that if the cravings didn't let up by 4pm I'd have a piece of nicotine gum or put on a patch. So for the next couple hours I surfed around on the computer and watched TV.

At 4pm I had that piece of nicotine gum. It tasted terrible, but it did ease the craving from a ten to about a six. The remainder of the day was the same. TV, laundry, snack, sleep. Sunday evening came. I wanted to smoke. I mean I really, really wanted to smoke. I surely didn't feel like a non-smoker yet. I felt like an addict without his fix.

But I'd made it through the weekend.

I might've felt the weekend had been a success were it not for the feeling there was a nail driven in my forehead and the intense desire for a cigarette.

But I didn't smoke at all that weekend, and I believe it was the steps I'd planned and followed that allowed me to make it through that first weekend smoke free and in a mental state of self-control.

I'd made another small step up the ladder and out of the swamp. I wasn't standing on the bottom anymore.

Me: 1   Swamp: 0

Chapter 8

Relapse

In the second chapter, I touched on the subject of relapses. In past attempts to quit, I'd relapse and have cheat cigarettes all the time. Quitting was already a miserable affair and cheat smokes were a guilty pleasure that temporarily eased the cravings.

But the relapses made me feel guilty which compounded the misery of life without full time smoking. Eventually, I'd decide that I was failing so much that I might as well just give in and start smoking full time again.

That was a mistake. I won't go so far as to say that everyone relapses. But I will say that I think most people who quit smoking have moments of weakness and they relapse. Admitting this beforehand was powerful. Admitting that, yes, there would be times I would be overcome with cravings and I'd slip up.

So I changed my expectations.

In past attempts to quit, I naively hoped I could do it without ever slipping. Every time I did cheat, I felt like I was another rung further down the ladder to complete failure.

But this time I went in with the knowledge that at some point I would more than likely cheat. It doesn't mean I gave myself a guilt-free pass to cheat whenever it got to be too much.

It did mean that I wouldn't use relapses as an excuse to give in and start smoking full-time again.

Since I was aware of the fact that at some point, I was likely going to relapse and have a cheat smoke, I needed a way to, at the very least, keep the cheating under control.

In the past, every time I'd quit, I'd bum a cigarette off anyone who had them, friends and co-workers included. This time I decided to make it harder on myself.

I had decided that during the first week or two after my detox weekend, I would allow myself to have a cheat cigarette any time I wanted.

That's right.

I would allow myself to cheat any time I needed to. But... there were a few caveats.

It was only as an absolute last resort, after willpower alone failed. After the patch and gum had failed. If it got so bad that I couldn't take it anymore. Then I would allow a relapse, but in some sort of controlled way.

This 'allowed relapse" idea created a problem though. If I bought cigarettes, relapse would surely turn into failure. Bumming cigarettes off my smoking friends and co-workers was too easy, and if it was too easy, it would also likely lead to failure.

Besides, I was limiting my exposure to my smoking friends, so that wouldn't work anyway. I needed to find a different way.

So I decided that I would only allow myself to bum a cigarette off a complete stranger. And I'd have to offer them money for it. And I had to smoke it in private, by myself.

I wanted there to be none of the social nurturing that goes with smoking a cigarette with other smokers. Plus, it's embarrassing to ask a stranger if you can buy a smoke from them, then turn down their offer to light it for you because you want to take it with you to smoke it in private.

Lastly, I could only have one cheat smoke per day, and I could not have them on consecutive days. And I could not have more than two per week. These are the rules I laid out for myself.

The Tuesday after I quit, I forgot all about motivation and getting rid of victim mentality. I wanted to smoke. I wanted to smoke so bad I could climb the walls.

Remembering my caveats, I drove around looking for some stranger who might be smoking. I wanted to call one of my buddies that smoked, but instead I drove to a gas station and paid two dollars for a single cigarette off the girl who works behind the counter.

I drove away and greedily inhaled cigarette smoke as deep as I could. At the time, I never regretted smoking it. What I did regret was that I didn't buy two cigs off her. But I stuck to my relapse plan and went home, determined to get back on the wagon.

It wasn't easy. This time I had no toothpicks, no bubble gum, no sunflower seeds or candy to keep my hands and mouth busy. I had temporarily abandoned my smoking friends, so I felt a little lonely and a little out of the social loop.

The smoking routines and habits in my life ran deep. My body would often act without me consciously thinking about it.

Every morning I got in my truck and I'd flip the sun-visor down out of habit, my fingers on autopilot, reaching around looking for a deck of smokes. That's where I kept my truck smokes. There was always a pack above the visor. But they weren't there anymore, and it took a long, long time, months in fact, for my fingers to break the habit of automatically reaching up there when I got in the truck.

Or I'd walk out of the office and turn around to go back in because I'd think I must've forgot my cigs on the desk. My hands were automatically reaching into my shirt pocket feeling for cigs when I walked out of the office. But my shirt pocket was now empty. No, it wasn't easy.

Everything reminded me of the cigarettes I wasn't smoking.

A few days later, I was on a jobsite. With smokers. Heavy smokers. Every coffee break was torture. I'd smell the smoke in the air and watch them smoking. These guys knew me well and asked why I wasn't smoking.

"I'm making an honest effort to cut back." I told them.

I broke my relapse rules that day. I bummed one cigarette from them at lunch. I had another at coffee break. I never paid them money for them either.

They were friends and wouldn't have taken any money anyway. On the way home from work, I smoked the last cigarette of my life. I admit it. I enjoyed every puff. And I smoked it right down to the nub. And I wanted another.

When I drove past a gas station on the way home, I was tempted. It was the same gas station I had given up, admitted defeat, and bought smokes at in the past. But this time I gritted my teeth drove right on by. I remember watching the gas station getting smaller and smaller in my rear view mirror. Part of me desperately wanted to turn around and go buy a pack of cigarettes.

But I didn't.

In those first few weeks following quit day, I'd had a number of relapse cigarettes. But having those silly little relapse rules did help, even though I eventually broke them.

Those silly little rules kept me honest for days at a time. If nothing else, they reminded me of my commitment to stay smoke free in spite of relapses. Reminded me that relapsing did not have to equal failure.

Eventually I started making better choices. When cravings were driving me crazy, I would do something positive, like exercise. I would recognize where my head was at mentally, acknowledge the miserable feelings of withdrawal and frustration, then force myself to think about something else and do something other than obsessing over the negative feelings.

The hardest days of craving, for me, were the first four or five. Really, that whole first week was pretty miserable. I wasn't feeling quite as bad as I had in past attempts though; that feeling of being an out of control locomotive.

I was following the plan that I'd laid out weeks earlier, so even though quitting was hard, I had a sense of direction and purpose that I believed would carry me through. And the fact that I'd weaned myself down before quit day helped immeasurably.

But I still had extreme mood swings, headaches and cravings. For some reason day eleven was really bad. I remember waking up every morning and being amazed that I'd actually made it another day. What a fantastic feeling.

Then day eleven comes along, and bang, it felt like day one all over again. I had a similar experience somewhere around the three week mark too.

It didn't suddenly get easy either. It was a process.

The first month was really, really hard. But each smoke free day, and I kept count of them, was just a bit easier than the day before.

Of course there were some days when I'd really have trouble with cravings, both mental and physical. On those days, I'd really have to focus and control how I handled my feelings and the discomfort of withdrawal.

Forget yesterday, forget tomorrow, just do whatever it takes to make it through that day. Those are the days that I wished I hadn't decided to keep my quitting private, that I could've called someone and just talked about it.

If I was to do it all over again, I probably would have picked at least one person whom I could have called on for support.

But in the end, it would be my own determination and willpower that was required to beat this thing, so I toughed it out. I remembered a conversation I had with this friend, Harry, who had quit cold turkey. He literally just threw his smokes out the window one day and never looked back.

When I asked him how he managed the cravings, he looked at me out of the corner of his eye and said matter of factly;

"I just toughed it out, what else are you gonna do?"

Even several months later, every time I saw a television show or movie where someone smoked, it felt like there was literally something itchy in my brain. And how easy a cigarette could scratch that itch.

The times I found myself around smokers was very hard that first year. I'd catch myself gazing at the cigarette in their fingers, and imagined what it'd be like to feel a cigarette between my fingers again. I'd imagine inhaling deeply.

The first months, I struggled with actual physical cravings. I think it took a year to get myself to the point where I didn't physically or mentally have cravings and longings for all the rituals.

In many ways, I had to reinvent myself and my life. To realize that I was actually a non-smoker now, and to replace the old routines and habits in my life with ones that are positive.

But I'm getting ahead of myself again and there's a lot I haven't talked about yet.

chapter 9

Friends

I remember when I finally spilled the beans to my friends that I'd quit.

They were shocked to learn that I hadn't smoked for two weeks. Most were impressed and very supportive. Still, I had a couple of those negative comments I mentioned at the beginning of the book. Both from smokers and non-smokers alike.

I have this one friend, a heavy smoker. He's a great guy. But just he didn't believe that I was smoke free. I'd hear through the grape vine that he thought I must be 'closet smoking', smoking behind everyone's back.

Before I quit, he and I used to get together for coffee and cigarettes quite often. We'd discuss work, politics, sports, you name it. All the while smoking and drinking lots of coffee.

Now that I'd quit, I was seeing him considerably less than usual. Not that I liked him any less, it's just that it was hard to be around him, watching him smoke. Then one evening, a group of us, all friends, went out for supper. At some point during the evening, the question was asked if I was still smoke free. I was.

When we left the restaurant, we stood in the parking lot and chatted for a few minutes before we all went our separate ways. This smoker friend lit a cigarette, and then handed it to me;

"Here, hold this for a second while I tie my shoe"

It was pretty obvious that he was either testing or tempting me. It was very strange to feel a cigarette in my finger-tips but I wasn't tempted at all. More disappointed in my friend for pulling such a stunt.

I had many smoking friends back when I was a smoker. It's not that I'm not friends with them anymore. But after I quit, I made some serious changes to my lifestyle. In the introduction to this book, I talked about not only leaving a negative lifestyle behind, but moving forward, making changes and living a positive life.

Now I was getting out and doing positive things with my life. I was eating well and exercising every day. Some of those smoking buddies, the ones I mainly used to sit around and drink coffee and smoke cigarettes with; they just faded out of my life a little bit.

There's this one guy I know. He used to call me and say;

"Let's go drink some coffee and smoke some cigarettes"

He's a great guy and still a friend. But we never get together for coffee and smokes anymore, so I see less of him.

He actually quit smoking for a couple years too. But he made the mistake of letting his guard down, letting the alligator back in the swamp.

He was going to weekly poker games where a lot of smoking was going on. Eventually, he succumbed and now he's smoking again full time.

For me, I just completely avoid activities and places where smoking is commonplace. Sure, it's not always possible. But that was part of the clean break, the change in lifestyle I made when I quit. Finding places to go and things to do that are healthy and smoke free.

It's a lot easier to beat temptation when you remove yourself from sources of temptation in the first place.

I remember a time, about a year after I quit smoking. I put this jacket on that I hadn't worn in ages. When I put my hands in the pockets, I found a lone cigarette.

I pulled it out, all dry and crusty.

But I didn't throw it away. I rolled it between my fingers. I held it in my lips, unlit. I smelled it. I thought about what it'd be like to light it up.

Then I walked to the trash can and crushed it, watching the dried tobacco fall from my hands. After a whole year of being smoke free, I didn't like that I actually considered lighting it. I realized that even after a year, I was still capable of being tempted, that the draw was still there.

Another fellow I know had quit smoking for over ten years.

His best friend was getting married and a bunch of guys went out on the town for his friend's stag party. For that one night he decided to have a few cigarettes to celebrate. He's smoking full time again. Sad.

Even my sister checks up on me from time to time. At a recent family barbeque, I ran out to the store to buy some sour cream for the baked potatoes. When she saw me drive up to the house, she asked if I'd snuck out for a smoke. I told her I hadn't smoked in years.

"Oh, I thought maybe you had started and were just closet smoking again"

What is it with that term? Closet smoking. The second time someone had accused me of it. Glad to say each time they were wrong.

There are times in everyone's life when we're around smokers and there's not much we can do about it.

Social functions, work, family gatherings, etc. It's easier to handle those times when we're exposed to cigarettes if it's the exception rather than the rule.

I'm a firm believer in limiting exposure to temptation. I may be a non-smoker now, but I am fully aware that the addictive part of my personality will always be vulnerable, to a certain degree anyway.

I want to keep the swamp drained and the alligator out, permanently. I really do feel for anyone that quits smoking and yet, say, lives with a spouse that continues to smoke. I can't imagine how hard that must be.

Hopefully if that's the case for you, you can at least find some areas of your life that remain a smoke free sanctuary. Maybe you can make a deal with your spouse to have part of the house a smoke free zone.

In this book I've talked a lot about the people that say and do things that are negative and detrimental to your efforts to live a smoke free life.

But there have also been so many people that have been inspirational in helping me quit. Some of the best and most helpful people were former smokers. They not only knew exactly what I was going through, but their advice was extremely useful.

I'd like to say thank you to each and every one of them for their words of inspiration and encouragement. All the fellows I mention here; I got a ton of inspiration and ideas from them. I owe a special thanks to these guys.

Harry. What a gem of a guy. Kind of a ruff and gruff no nonsense type of fellow who'd grown up on a ranch, worked with his hands, but with a sense of humor and a personality that just shone. He used to run heavy equipment when he was alive, and he told me that after a lifetime of smoking, he got fed up one day and threw his cigarettes out the window of the bulldozer he was operating. It was that simple for him. Sheer determination.

Lane. He's a college friend that told me how he quit smoking by weaning himself down one cigarette a day until he no longer smoked. He also told me that no one, not even his wife knew that he'd quit until several weeks after he'd done so. His story inspired me to make those things part of my own quit smoking process. He was smoke-free for years. Unfortunately, when he hit a few of life's speed bumps, he returned to smoking after 8 years of living without them.

Caleb. He's the guy behind the t-shirt; *I'll try anything once…maybe twice*. A fantastic dude and a great friend. Our many conversations about living an addiction free lifestyle and having an addiction free mindset were invaluable. He is still living a fantastic addiction free life today.

David. That's the guy that used to call me and say "Let's smoke some cigarettes and drink some coffee." He's also the one who told me that when he quit smoking, he would hole up in the house for a few days to get away from it all. Also something I incorporated into my own plan.

Gordon. He's the guy who'd be on the patch for months at a time, then switch back to smokes, then back to the patch again. He lived like that for years. I'm happy to report that he is now living completely nicotine free.

To all of these people, and so many more. Thank you! If it were not for them, I wouldn't be smoke free today.

Meeting people that had both succeeded and failed at staying smoke-free was extremely influential for me.

Learning what things worked for others that might work for me. And learning to recognize addictive behavior and pitfalls also became an important tool in the fight for an addiction free life.

In the long term, staying smoke-free day to day, week to month to year requires dedication and determination. The places you go and people you surround yourself with can be very influential on your ability to maintain a smoke-free lifestyle.

Becoming a non-smoker is more than just becoming someone who no longer puts cigarettes into their mouth. I believe it requires some life changes as well. It requires that you make proper, informed choices in your behavior and your response to circumstances. The result of all your choices is where you find yourself in your life today.

I leave you with this final thought about friends.

If your friends resist your lifestyle changes, want you to be a certain type of individual, or do things that impede your ability to achieve and maintain your smoke-free lifestyle, then you possibly need to re-evaluate those relationships.

As best as you can, I believe you should surround yourself with positive people who have positive goals regarding health and life in general.

Chapter 10

My list

As I write this chapter, more than four years have passed since the last time I lit a cigarette.

It feels really good to be a non-smoker, but for the most part, it's a non-issue now. It's been three years since I've had any real physical nicotine cravings and I cannot remember the last time I've had a mental craving.

Still, even now I avoid places where there's smoking. Not just because I don't like smoking, but I've seen too many guys who had it beat and slipped back into the smoking lifestyle because they got careless.

So I ask myself why?

Why did it work this time for me? Of all the other times I attempted to quit and failed, why did it work this time?

There's really nothing in this book that hasn't been written about or tried before.

No magic bullet. No quick and easy fix.
Why did it work this time? Why am I free?

The day I got serious and decided I would find a way to quit started with a process of self examination, and that involved writing things down. I ended up keeping a journal throughout the process, and that journal became this book.

Thus far this book has been sort of autobiographical, my journal of the journey I took from smoker to non-smoker. But now I'm going to try to break down what I think were the most important tools I used and steps I took to break free from smoking, and put it into point form for you.

I believe any good stop smoking program is like a map or pathway of sorts. One in which the average person can follow and consistently achieve better than average results.

It should contain easily recognizable steps to follow, that will lead you out of the abyss of addiction and to a life of freedom.

So here is my list, my map. I believe following this map is the reason I finally succeeded at giving up cigarettes for good.

1.   Self-examination.

I spent some time examining my life, and considering just how intertwined smoking had become in my life. I sat down with a pen and a notebook and just wrote things down, all the areas of my life that involved smoking. It was a long list.

It's not that I ever planned to have my life revolve around smoking, but that's how it had become. From the friends I spent the most time with, to the activities and hobbies I chose, almost everything in my life was very closely associated with smoking.

I mean, I couldn't just make a quick trip to the grocery store to buy a loaf of bread before supper. I'd have to have a cigarette on the way to the store too. When it came down to it, my daily routine and my social structure was firmly structured around smoking cigarettes.

Of course, on some level, I knew all this beforehand. But taking the time to analyze this and to recognize just how deeply engrained smoking was in my life. I realized that if I was ever going to really succeed at quitting, I'd have to do more than stop putting cigarettes in my mouth.

My life needed an overhaul too.

Ok, it's your turn. Write down some of your biggest smoking **triggers**. These are the things make you say "I need a smoke!"

Stress at work, the kids are fighting *again*, the car is making a funny noise and you can't afford any unexpected bills right now, etc. Everyone has things that trigger them. Let's list some of the things that trigger you most often.

_____

_____

_____

_____

_____

_____

Now examine your addictive **routines**. Routines are not the same as triggers. Routines are your daily habits and patterns that revolve around smoking. For me, having a cigarette after every meal was one of my many smoking routines.

You need to be able to identify negative routines before you can change or eliminate them. List the people, places, activities and things that you associate most with smoking.

_____

_____

_____

_____

_____

_____

2. Talk to successful people.

I talked to people who had successfully stopped smoking, and I took the parts of their success story that was a fit for me, and implemented it into my own plan.

It was a process of cherry picking what worked for them and recognizing which of those things might work for me, even if it meant I had to modify their ideas to my own needs and circumstances.

Your turn. Write down a few **people** you know who've successfully quit smoking. Wanna give them a call?

_____

_____

_____

_____

3. Come up with a plan.

I'm not saying my plan was any better than any other stop-smoking plan out there. But the fact that I'd spent some time analyzing why I'd failed in the past set me up for success.

By identifying the things that caused me to fail, I could formulate a plan that would allow me to avoid the very things that had tripped me up in the past.

Having a plan, a map to follow, gave me a sense of purpose and a feeling of control. Quitting became less of a feeling of giving something up, and more of a mission, something that I might be able to conquer.

I made my plan pretty specific. It included a timeline that began several weeks before the actual quit day and extended well past the actual quit day.

I tried to include contingency plans for everything; from what I would do with nicotine cravings to how I was going to handle being around other smokers, to what I'd do when I relapsed, etc.

There were two main areas of focus in my plan.

a) Breaking the actual physical addiction to nicotine as quickly possible. I am a firm believer that aids such as the patch, nicotine gum, or medication can help you quit.

But in every one of my past attempts to quit, I had never completely removed nicotine from my life. I had never actually broken the physical addiction before. Nicotine always remained after I 'quit'. Either in the form of the patch or nicotine gum or cheat cigarettes.

This time would be different.

b) I would address my psychological addiction. This meant restructuring the way I lived my life, the places I spent time at, the people I hung around with. I knew that even if I succeeded in quitting, it wouldn't last if I kept trying to live my life the same way I was when I smoked.

This time, I would give my life an overhaul.

Your turn again. Time to start scratching down a few ideas on how you'll put your plan into action. Don't worry, it doesn't have to be perfect. It just has to work for you.

For every trigger you wrote down in step 1, write down something you could do to neutralize those triggers. How will you modify your life to eliminate addictive habits and routines?

_____

_____

_____

_____

_____

4. Approach quitting like you are in control.

There are times in our lives where it seems like we're not in control of what's going on around us.

Our obligations with work, family, friends, debt, etc, require our time, energy, and effort. Quite often it may feel like our job or boss, or even our personal debt or life circumstances are controlling a very large portion of our lives.

Once you quit smoking, the very crutch you leaned on to help you cope with these obligations will be gone, possibly leaving you feeling like your life is even more out of control.

But it is imperative that you face quitting like you are in control of your life and your body. Having and following a plan, as well as the other items on this list are tools to help you maintain that control.

Don't be pushed around by cravings or your old habits. *You* are in control of *you.*

Write this down: *I am in control.*

Now, say it out loud. Twice!

5. Set a date and actively prepare yourself in the weeks before that date.

Quitting doesn't begin after you smoke your last cigarette. It begins in the weeks before, when you start putting your plan into action.

I weaned myself down in the weeks prior to my quit day. This was a crucial step. The weeks before hand, where I weaned myself down, was like being in training for the main event.

Over those weeks prior to actually quitting, I had lowered the number of cigarettes I smoked daily. I even had several 24 hour periods where I had gone without smoking any cigarettes.

Lowering my bodies daily nicotine threshold meant that those first four or five days after I quit were a lot easier to handle.

Some may look at quit day as the day you start breaking the actual physical addiction. But those weeks where I weaned myself down, that was really the first step to breaking the physical addiction my body had for nicotine.

Once quit day actually came, I did my very best to eliminate every form of nicotine from my body. I wanted the physical part of the addiction handled as soon as possible.

I had mentally toughened myself up in those weeks, and instead of considering quit day as 'doomsday', I looked at it like a challenge, and obstacle to overcome. Something I had been training for.

Your turn: Go ahead. Get your calendar out. Take a look at your schedule. (I'll just wait here until you're ready)

So when is it? Which day is going to be Q-day?

_____

Great!! You've got some work to do and some preparations to make before Q-day. But you're on your way.

6. You need to be willing to make some changes in your life routine.

After living so many years with cigarettes, facing a new life without them can seem like stepping into deep uncharted waters.

The unknown can be frightening in any circumstance, and even with a solid action plan that addresses most of your stumbling blocks, actually living that plan will, at times, leave you feeling very uncertain. The draw to go back to your old comfortable way of living will loom large.

But if you are going to break free from smoking, you need to open yourself up to changing the way you live. To welcome the unknown. To truly be willing to change your lifestyle without continually questioning or complaining about the changes.

You need to have a willingness to change.

Repeat after me:
I am willing to do whatever it takes to make this happen because I'm not going to live as an addict anymore.

7. On quit day, make a definite break from your life routine.

I believe this was probably the most crucial step in being able to break free from smoking permanently.

I had examined and analyzed what many of my weaknesses were. Knowing that many of those weaknesses were associated with my daily routine and my social structure gave me the impetus to make some drastic changes.

That's why I isolated myself from the world that first weekend. It's why I scoured my house and my vehicle and removed everything that I associated with smoking. It's why I completely isolated myself from other smokers for the first few days after I had officially quit.

I wanted a singularity of purpose for those first few days, and so I tried to eliminate the most obvious obstacles that might trip me up. I holed up in the house, away from everything and took on the addiction without any outside interference.

When I was tired and lethargic, I could sleep without it affecting any other part of my life.

I don't recommend eating junk food and starting another bad habit when you quit. But having a temporary junk food indulgence over that first weekend was something my addictive mind-set needed. A temporary crutch, so to speak.

That weekend was the beginning of a new life and a new lifestyle for me. Breaking my old, addictive routine extended well beyond that first weekend. It continued from then until this very day.

I did not want to merely stop smoking, and yet try to continue living my life the same old way. That wouldn't work. There would be a huge hole in my life, one that cigarettes had previously filled.

I needed to fill that hole with positive things, develop coping skills, adjust my daily routines and social patterns, and create positive non-addictive relationships.

To an outsider, things may or may not have seemed to change all that much.

But for me, the change in my life routine was extremely important in staying smoke free.

Your turn: You've picked out a **Quit-Day**. It's time to plan out what that day will look like. What time will you quit? What will you do about work and family obligations? Are there headache tablets in case you get a headache?

Here's a sample Q-day plan to get you started:
- Smoke last cigarette at _____
- Search through the house and car; find all cigarettes, ashtrays, and anything related to smoking and throw them out.
- Go buy groceries. Healthy stuff and some treats too.
- Find a healthy recipe and make a delicious, nutritious supper.
- Take a long walk.
- Binge watch Netflix for a few hours before bed.

I could go on and on.

The more detailed your plan, the more control you will feel. Being able to check items off your list as your Q-day unfolds will make you feel empowered and give you a sense of accomplishment.

My List

8.   You need to be willing to go through nicotine withdrawal.

It's going to be uncomfortable, for a while. You need to be ok with that.

I know there are some stop smoking programs out there that promise you'll be able to quit without any discomfort or withdrawals.

I'm sorry, but I just can't make that kind of claim here. I believe that regardless of what steps you take and what addiction aids you use, there is going to be a certain amount of discomfort when you stop smoking. At times it sucks, plain and simple.

There are smoking cessation medications and nicotine aids like patches and gum that can help minimize withdrawal symptoms. Mentally, there are a few different ways to deal with withdrawal discomfort too.

You can try blocking the discomfort out and pretending it doesn't exist, acting like everything in your life is just fine. But in reality the discomfort does exist.

You can try to fight the feelings of discomfort, take them on and struggle against them and try to *will* them into submission. But for me, fighting the discomfort eventually left me physically and mentally exhausted while the discomfort remained.

But there is another option.

There will be times when you'll need to quiet your internal dialogue and stop obsessing about how lousy you're feeling in the moment.

Not to deny the anxiety, withdrawals or fear, but to admit and submit to those feelings and embrace them. You'll need to endure the personal discomfort of withdrawal and life-change with a sense of willingness and, just as importantly, with a sense of detachment.

When I was in my early twenties, I was in a really bad accident. I was in the hospital for a month and underwent several operations. I'm still partially disabled from that accident today. Despite being given some of the strongest painkillers, I was in excruciating pain for weeks at a time.

During my hospital stay, I developed some mental tricks that helped me cope with the pain.

I transferred and used these little tricks and coping methods when I was faced with heavy nicotine withdrawal cravings.

Similar to when I was in pain in the hospital, I found that when the nicotine withdrawals and cravings were really bad, it helped if I described to myself exactly what I was feeling, from head to toe. I described it to myself as if I was trying to explain what I was feeling to my doctor.

I vividly described the location, size, color, shape, temperature, and texture of the discomfort. I would even rate the discomfort on a scale of one to ten. Then I allowed myself to accept and experience those feelings of discomfort.

I found when I did that, much of the power and energy drained away from those negative feelings, and I was able to manage living with the discomfort.

Instead of continually obsessing over and fighting the feelings of discomfort, I embraced them. Then I got on with my day with the realization that for now, and for just a little while into my future, they were part of my reality.

These are some of the coping skills I used. I found that if I consciously chose my thoughts and my response to those feelings of discomfort, I retained a greater feeling of control over my life.

Just know that there is a certain amount of discomfort that is unavoidable when you stop smoking, and you must be willing to experience it.

Your turn: I put a mechanism into my plan so that when the door to relapse showed up, I'd have a way to handle it. I have to admit, going out and buying a single cigarette to prevent total relapse probably wasn't the best idea, even though it did work for me.

Take a minute to think about the last times you tried to quit, and those moments when you relapsed.

Write down here, or on a sheet of paper, the circumstances that led you to relapsing the last time you tried to stop smoking.

Describe the emotions going through your head in the hours prior to lighting up that relapse smoke.

Now that you've identified what those moments of relapse look like, what are you going to do when they reappear in the future?

_____

_____

_____

_____

_____

_____

_____

9. Control the sources of temptation.

Especially in the beginning, when you first quit.

I severely restricted the amount of time I spent around smokers in those first few weeks. Even now, I never hang out with smokers while they are smoking.

Like I mentioned earlier;
- Remove the temptation,
- Remove yourself from the temptation,
- Develop new ways to manage yourself in the face of temptation.

10. Make positive changes in your life.

After I quit smoking I changed my life in numerous ways. Some of them seemingly small and insignificant, others more substantial. Part of my plan was to start doing positive things with my time and with my life.

Smokers are usually great conversationalists, sitting around and talking about all manner of things while they smoke cigarettes.

Throughout my smoking years, I had become one of those conversmokalists. But after I stopped smoking, I wanted to return to a more active lifestyle. One that included doing active, healthy things. This meant replacing many of my usual habits and pastimes with positive, more constructive things.

There's a whole big wide world out there, full of wonders and interests for everyone. It's almost limitless.

Whether it's just taking the dog for a daily walk, spending a Saturday afternoon in the park, hiking in the wild, or training for a 10K run. Taking a cooking, art or dance class or learning how to fix the carburetor on the lawnmower.

It could be volunteering, exercising, reading a book, or doing some travelling.

Just getting out there and doing positive things yields internal rewards and gives your life a purpose and meaning.

Plus you get to meet all sorts of other people who are out there doing fantastic things and living a non-addictive lifestyle.

Stopping smoking is your opportunity to make some fantastic positive changes in the way you live.

Your turn: It's time to make a list of some new positive healthy habits that you'll make when you become a non-smoker. New positive routines that will replace the old negative ones.

_____

_____

_____

_____

_____

_____

So once again, here is my list, my map:

1. Self Examination.

2. Learn from successful people.

3. Come up with a plan that suits your life.

4. Approach quitting like you are in control.

5. Set a date and actively prepare yourself in the weeks before.

6. Have a willingness to change your life routines.

7. On quit day, make a definite break from your life routine.

8. Have a willingness go through withdrawal.

9. Control the sources of temptation.

10. Make positive changes.

Chapter 11

Final thoughts

For years I used to tell myself that 'someday' in the future, I would quit smoking. But year after year, I continued to smoke. Quitting was always lost somewhere in the fog of the future.

One of the most powerful things I can tell you about the future is that there is nothing certain about tomorrow. All you have is right now. Today.

You can make all sorts of goals and plans for the future, but they will never become actualized until you take action and make them real in the here and now.

You can remain a slave to smoking. A victim controlled by the addiction, using smoking as a crutch to muddle your way through life. Or you can take responsibility for the addiction and make the required changes in your personal thoughts and behavior that will lead you to freedom and control of your life.

Quitting smoking and making all those changes, big and small, was not easy for me. In fact, it was some of the small idiosyncrasies that were hardest to give up or replace.

Driving to work without going through the daily ritual of opening a fresh pack of cigarettes, pulling one out, and lighting it was hard.

It seems silly, but no longer having a lit cigarette to roll in my fingers and fiddle with while I drank coffee took a long, long time to get used to.

But all of it; going through the nicotine withdrawals, making life changes, choosing my thoughts and behavior, developing coping skills. It gradually got better. I was slowly morphing into a non-smoker.

Each day was just a little bit easier than the one before. The discomfort I thought I could barely manage the previous week became increasingly easier to cope with the next week and in fact, was starting to diminish in a real way.

Eventually I realized that I was no longer struggling to live a life without cigarettes.

Far from it, I was living a life free of them. A life much fuller than it had ever been. I'd not only regained my health, but my life as well.

There are so many good books, programs and websites out there that are designed to help you quit smoking for good. Educate yourself. Read a bunch of those books.

Take what you learn and mold it into a plan that fits your own life and circumstances.

See your doctor.

My doctor was extremely helpful and supportive to me. He's the only one who knew I was quitting right from the start.

Looking back, I wish I'd chosen one or two non-judgmental, supportive people that I could've talked to for support through the process. That's something I recommend you do.

And talk to people who've done it, who've quit.

I think that'll probably be the best form of help you'll ever receive. Learning from those who've already walked the path you intend on taking.

Even if what I've written isn't a help to you, I hope that you persist. That you find a way.

I cannot express how liberating it's been for me to finally be free from the slavery of smoking. To be able to move past that and start living a life without addictions.

It's my hope that you can read this book and take something from it. Create a plan of your own. Something that fits your life and your circumstances and your personality.

So you can overhaul your life. Drain the swamp. Quit smoking. Become free.

I wish you all the best.

www.ingramcontent.com/pod-product-compliance
Lightning Source LLC
Chambersburg PA
CBHW030156070426
42447CB00031B/478